Lessons in Responsibility

(Once-A-Week Curriculum)

Level One

Lessons in Responsibility

This book is dedicated to all the fathers and mothers who diligently seek to train their children in the Lord our God, through the love of Jesus, their Messiah.

PEARABLES
P.O. Box 272000
Fort Collins, CO 80527

www.pearables.com

Instructions

Dear Parent,

We would like to welcome you to our new **Christian Gentleman's Series - Lessons in Responsibility**! So many beloved believers, like yourself, desire with all their hearts that their boys will grow up to be strong men of God. In the world around us we may see many young men who reflect a lack of responsibility in most areas of their lives. These young men will grow up to be tomorrow's adults.

It is our duty as parents to take the time to train young lads in the teachings of our Heavenly Father's Word. The main thing our Savior, Jesus, taught was to first be responsible towards the Father. The first thing in learning responsibility is to teach boys to first, love the Lord their God will ALL their hearts, ALL their souls, ALL their minds, and with ALL their strength. This is what this curriculum is all about. It will instill that loving God first means to be responsible to Him. When boys are responsible towards their Heavenly Father, they will then be responsible toward everyone else around them.

Responsibility training starts at home, gently and wooingly placed in the heart of young boys. We pray that **Lessons in Responsibility** will be an encouragement and help as you start your journey with your son.

The following suggestions may be of help:

1. This is a once-a-week program. This means that if dad (or mom!) is able to sit down with their son for about one hour a week, the young lad will be able to do the rest of the week's tasks all by himself as he completes his lesson.

2. Please remember to remind your son to continue using his skills which he will have learned the previous weeks. Lessons in Responsibility is just like training any other skill. They must practice it again and again and again until it becomes natural to them.

3. Once this book is completed, if you see that your child needs more review in some areas, please feel free to start all over again! Just as reading the Bible once is never enough, these Biblical and practical suggestions may need to be reviewed again. Don't go on to the next level until you feel your child is ready. It's not about completing a book. It's about having them truly learn and apply the contents of a lesson.

4. Lastly, enjoy this special time with your son. Remember, they grow up so quickly. Smile, laugh and share your joy with him as you learn along with them!

Much love in our Lord and Savior,

PEARABLES

✤ Level One ✤
CONTENTS

Jesus said unto him, "Thou shalt love the Lord thy God with ALL thy heart, and with ALL thy soul and with all thy mind, and with all thy strength, this is the first commandment."
Mark 12:30

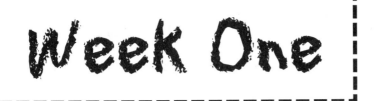

Responsibility

This is Ben. Ben is learning to be responsible, just like you!

At first he didn't know what the word RESPONSIBLE or RESPONSIBILITY meant, so he asked his dad to look it up in the dictionary. Can you ask your dad or mom to look it up for you?

What did you find? Ben found that it means that a responsible boy is a boy who can make good decisions on his own. It means that you can be trusted to do something someone asks of you, even if you have to do it all alone.

Who is the most important person to you in all the universe? Well, Ben thinks the most important is God, or Heavenly Father, and His Son, Jesus, and the Holy Spirit. He wants to learn to be responsible towards God. In other words, he wants to DO what his Heavenly Father wants him to do.

What do you think is the most important thing we can do for God?

Jesus answered this question in Mark 12:29-30. He said, "The Lord our God is one Lord; and thou (you) shall love the Lord your God with **all** your heart, and with **all** your soul, and with **all** your mind and with **all** your strength. This is the first commandment."

Before we can be responsible in other things, we first need to be responsible towards God.

Jesus told us that we are to love God with ALL of our being.

Can you obey this Scripture?

TASK: Sit with mom or dad and answer and discuss these questions.

1. How do you love the Lord your God with ALL of your heart?

2. How do you love the Lord your God with ALL of your soul?

3. How do you love the Lord your God with all of your mind?

4. How do you love the Lord your God with all of your strength?

5. How do you become responsible towards God? (The Scripture answers this for you.)

Let us love one another; for love is of God; and every one
that loveth is born of God, and knoweth God.
1 John 4:7

Week Two

Responsibility Through Love

God tells us that He wants us to love Him with ALL our hearts. Ben loves God with all his heart, but he wanted to know if he loved God with all his heart, how would there be room to love his mom, dad, family and friends?

When you love God with ALL your heart, he fills you up with His love so that you are able to love others even MORE! He miraculously makes even more room in your heart so that you can love how He loves.

When you love someone you will want to do what they tell you to do.

God says, "If you love me, you will do my Commandments." What is a commandment? It is a command. God is a King and He gives us rules to follow. His orders are found in the Bible.

Responsibility starts at home. If you love God, you will want to do what He tells you to do. One of the commands He wants us to follow is the one which tells us to obey and honor our parents.

Just like loving God, if you love your parents, you will want to do what your parents tell you to do.

This is a very important rule: **Always obey and honor your parents.**

Sometimes you may not like what your parents tell you to do. You may not agree with what they tell you. But just like our Heavenly Father, they are telling you these things for your own good.

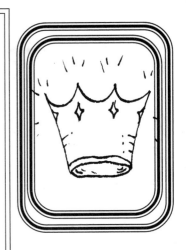

TASK: Sit down with your mom or dad and ask them to make some rules for you to follow. Ask them to make a list of "Household rules". Once the household rules are listed, try to do the following this week:

1. Memorize by heart what your household rules are.

2. Try to keep track of all the times you obey the rules and any time you break them.

3. At the end of the week, sit with dad or mom and answer this question:

Which did you do most often:

1. Obey the rules?

2. Disobey the rules?

3. Are you having a difficult or easy time learning to be responsible?

4. Discuss any rules you feel were unnecessary, and explain why.

Let all things be done decently and in order.
1 Corinthians 14:40

Week Three

Responsible
in
Heart

Responsibility & Your Belongings

Ben has an awful lot of stuff. Sometimes he forgets to be thankful for his things. When this happens, he doesn't pick up his room and it becomes very messy. He may leave his clothes all over his bedroom floor. This doesn't happen very often now. See, Ben is learning to be responsible towards all the things God has given him.

You, too, can learn to be responsible for your things. It's very easy to do.

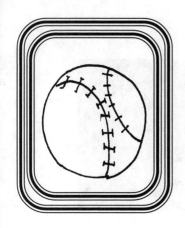

Let's go over a few things that Ben has learned which has helped him to keep his room in order and his stuff put up.

1. In your room, find a place to put your belongings. If you don't have something, ask your parents for a toy bin, baskets, or shelf that you can have for your very own. Once you have your space, decide where you are going to put your belongings! Here's a picture of what Ben did:

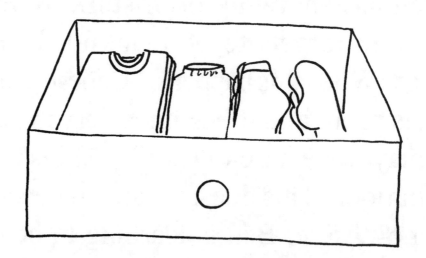

2. In your drawers, organize your clothing so that they have a special place to go. Ben puts his PJ's, underware, and socks in his top drawer. He puts his shirts in his

middle drawer. In the bottom drawer he placed his pants, sweaters and sweatshirts.

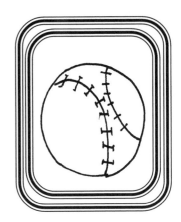

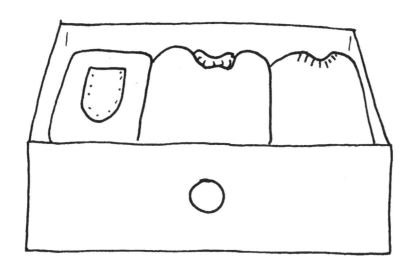

TASK: This week it is your turn to find a place for everything you own. Remember the saying, "Everything has a place and everything in its place!"

Once you have decided where all your things go, you will have a very easy time putting things up and keeping your room clean!

Keep your room picked up each day. You can do this! You are becoming responsible!

The steps of a good man are ordered by the Lord; and he delighten in his way.
Psalms 37:23

Week Four

Responsible in Heart

Responsibility & Your Bed

Who sleeps in your bed? Why YOU do! Are you big enough to make your own bed yet? Ben is going to show you how he makes his own bed each morning. He also has learned to changed his own sheets once a week!

Changing your sheets is very important as germs can collect on your sheets and cause you to become ill if you do not change them.

You are going to be surprised at how easy it is to change sheets and make a bed.

messy

Step 1: Put the fitted sheet in the middle of your bed with the short sides towards the ends.

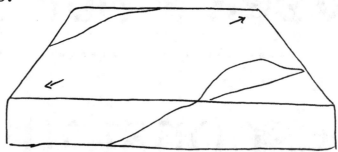

Step 2: Pull the opposite sides down over the corners of the bed. Complete pulling all edges of the right corners.

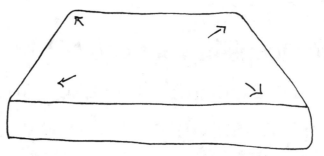

Step 3: Take the top sheet and evenly tuck the bottom sheet under the end of the bed.

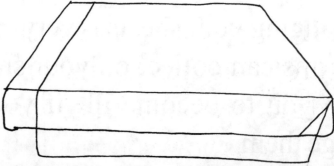

Step 4: Take your top blanket and pull

over the top of your bed. Stuff the bottom under the end like you did your top sheet. Tuck in all the sides.

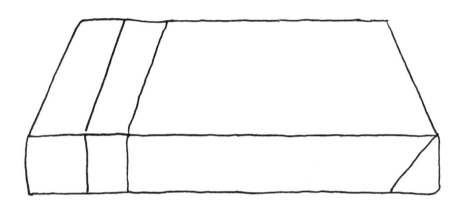

Step 5: Place your pillow on top and you are finished!

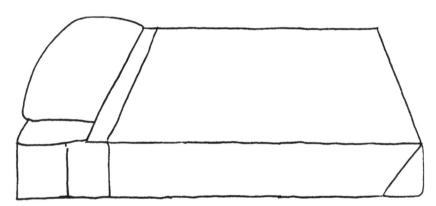

TASK: Every day make your bed, making sure your sheets and blankets are tucked nicely around the bottom and side edges. This is how you should leave your bedroom every morning.

Lessons in Responsibility

And I have given you cleanness of teeth in all your cities...
Amos 4:6

Week Five

Responsibility & Your Morning Routine

Now that you know how to make your bed and clean your room, you are more than ready to have a morning routine!

What's a morning routine? It's something that you do every morning.

Everyone has some type of morning routine, even if their routine is to never make their bed!

But you have learned how to be responsible in that area, haven't you?!

The following is a very simple morning routine. All you have to do is to complete the following steps:

Step 1. When you get up in the morning, after you go to the bathroom, come back to your room and make your bed. You should now be very good at making your own bed!

Step 2. After your bed is made, pick up and put away all the clothes that are around your room. This includes the PJ's you have just taken off..

Step 3. Put away any toys or play items you may have overlooked.

Step 4. Go into the bathroom and wash your hands and face, brush your teeth, and comb your hair. Make sure to put everything away after you are done.

TASK: This week try to follow all your steps every morning. If you can do it each day this week, you are on your way to-wards becoming responsible! Hurray!

Helpful Tip:

Ben's mom and dad helped him to make a chore board. Whenever he completed his steps, he was able to draw or glue a nice star in a box on his board. Soon he had a whole page of stars and, boy, did he feel great! He could see what he had achieved!

Chore Board:

Ben's Steps				
Bed	clothes	toys	face	teeth
❋	❋	❋	❋	❋
❋	❋	❋	❋	❋
❋	❋	❋	❋	❋
❋	❋	❋	❋	❋
❋	❋	❋	❋	❋
❋	❋	❋	❋	❋

Lessons in Responsibility

Be kindly affectioned one to another with brotherly love;
in honor preferring one another.
Romans 12:10

Week Six

Responsibility & Your Siblings

What's a *sibling*? Siblings are your brothers and your sisters. God calls all children blessings. You are a blessing and so are your brothers and sisters. How are you supposed to treat your family members?

Ben has three brothers and one sister. When you love God with ALL your heart, you are going to love what He has given you. Ben is so thankful that God loved him so much that he gave him his family. He wants to be a very good brother.

Ben doesn't mean to be selfish, however, he sometimes thinks of his own needs and wants before the wishes of his family. Has this ever happened to you?

For example, one day his sister wanted to listen to one of her songs on the CD player in the house. Ben had been listening to his music and didn't want to turn it off yet. What would be the kind thing for Ben to have done? Yes, it would be very good of him to have given his sister a turn.

The point is to GIVE... GIVE a turn, GIVE a helping hand, GIVE up something. God loves a cheerful giver.

It is so important to learn to be responsible towards your brothers and sisters. If you can't be kind to them at home when no one is watching, you are not going to learn to be a responsible and kind family member yourself. How you treat your siblings is how you will treat your own family when you grow up.

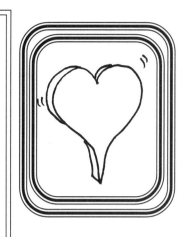

TASK: Be responsible towards your brothers and sisters this week. This means that you will interact with them with the knowledge that God is watching. Are you loving them with ALL your heart? When we aren't loving *others* with all our hearts, we probably aren't loving God with ALL our hearts either.

1. Keep an open eye. Each day look for ways to help each of your siblings *at least twice!* Do they need help or your support doing a chore? Do they look sad or angry....? If so, give them a smile or a hug. Tell dad or mom what you have done each day. Tell Father God what you have done and ask Him to help you see more ways to help them.

2. Write on a list, one thing that you are going to do for each of your brothers and sisters this week. Don't let them know you are going to do this.

Parents, talk with your child about protecting their older and younger family members. It can be either physically watching out for them, or spiritually. These little ones' hearts are so precious yet so fragile.

Jesus said, "Let the little ones come unto me."

Lessons in Responsibility

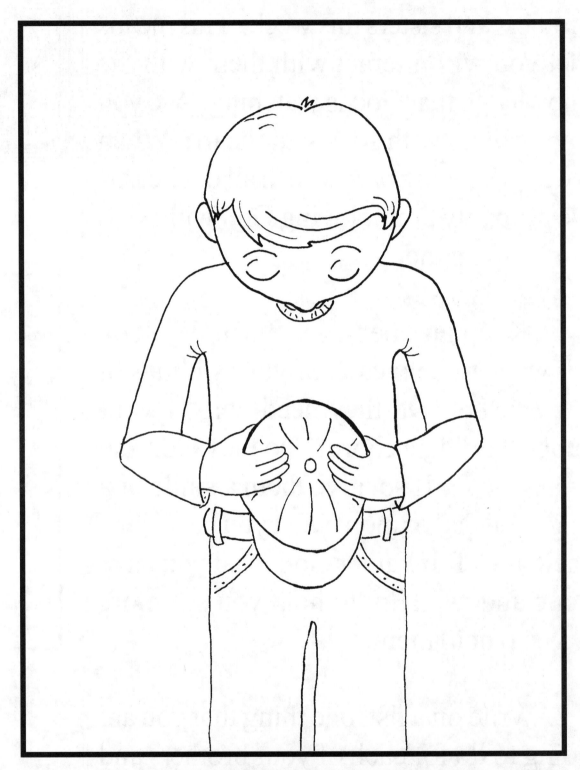

Finally, be ye all of one mind, having compassion one of another, love as brethren, be pitiful, be courteous.
1 Peter 3:8

Week Seven

Responsible in Heart

Responsibility If You Have a Sister

As a young boy, you need to understand that your sisters are much different than you are. As a boy, you are also to be responsible for your sister as her protector.

Ben has one sister who is older than him, but he does the best he can to take care of her.

He has found out that she is much more frail than his brothers. She hurts herself if

she plays as hard as boys do. She used to try to keep up with them in sports, but she broke too many bones and had to quit.

God made sisters quite wonderfully. You must remember that they are very different from you. They cry, get their feelings hurt, and show their emotions more than most boys. They are also made smaller and more delicate than boys. This is where you come in. If you can see that your sister is in trouble in any way, it is your responsibility to go and help her.

Whether your sisters are younger or older than you are, you need to keep an eye on them. Love your sisters with your actions.

TASK: This week try the following ideas in order to learn how to be responsible towards your sister. (If you don't have a sister, then do this towards your mother.)

1. Bring your sisters flowers or a treat

that will brighten up their day.

2. Tell your sister that you want to play with her for a while.

3. Help your sister if she is carrying something that is heavy. Remember, girls are sometimes more delicate than you are. Most boys are built so much stronger than girls are.

4. Keep your sister protected from other boys. Keep your eyes on your sister and make sure that you are right there when she needs you.

5. Protect your sister and all other girls. Never, ever hit or hurt a girl physically in any way, shape, or form.

6. Talk with your dad or mom about how you should treat your sister when you get angry with her.

Lessons in Responsibility

Children, obey your parents in the Lord; for this is right.
Ephesians 6:1

Week Eight

Responsibility & Your Parents

You are so very lucky! You have your parents helping you to grow into a responsible young man!

Sadly, there are many young lads who do not have someone helping them to grow into young men of God. They are left to themselves as they try to find out what it means to be a man. Television will not tell them how to be a Godly man. Music on the radio will not tell them the correct

way to be a Godly man.

Do you know what will tell you how to be a Godly man? Yes, The BIBLE! Your parents are reading the Bible and are try-ing teach you what it says to do to live a life that will glorify God. We talked a while ago about obeying and honoring your mom and dad.

Do you obey your parents? Some of the time? All of the time?

When your parents give you instruction, are they doing it because they don't like you? No! They are taking the time to tell you things so that you will be safe.

God does this too. When He tells us to obey certain commands or rules in His Word, the Bible, He tells us these things so that we will remain safe.

****

Ben learned this the hard way. He was on the sidewalk riding his skateboard. His dad had told him to never jump off the edge of the sidewalk into the street.

One day he didn't think anyone was watching and he decided to not obey his dad. He got up some speed and then hit the edge. He went flying one way onto the sidewalk. His skateboard went flying the other way into the street. Along came an unseen car and it ran right over Ben's board. That skateboard was demolished right in front of his eyes. He sure wished he had obeyed his dad.

Parents, Read Exodus 20:12 to your son. Remind him about the promise with this scripture if it is obeyed.

TASK: Discuss with your dad or mom what it means to honor them. Have dad look up HONOR in the dictionary and read Exodus 20:12 with him.

This week try to honor your parents every single day. See if you can go all week long without dishonoring them. You can do it!

The Dictionary definition of HONOR: 1. Esteem, respect, reverence.

A man that has friends must show himself friendly; and there
is a friend that sticketh closer than a brother.
Proverbs 18:24

Week Nine

Responsible in Heart

Responsibility & Your Friends

Aren't friends a wonderful thing? I bet you have a few good friends, don't you?

Ben has friends, but he has had to learn how to treat them. Jesus told us, "Do to others as you would have them do to you."

Sometimes Ben didn't want to share his toys with his friends. When this happened his friends didn't want to be around him for a while because he was being too selfish.

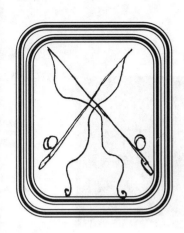

As Ben has learned to share, all of his friends love to play with him now.

Sometimes we forget to treat others kindly. Have you ever done this?

In order to remember how to treat his friends, Ben's mother made up a reminder list to help him:

F is for being FAIR

R is for RESPECTING others

I is for having INTEGRITY

E is for being an EXAMPLE

N is for behaving NICELY

D is for DUTY towards others

S is for SHARING

H is for HONOR

I is for IGNORING wrongs

P is for PRAISING others good traits

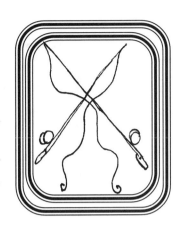

Did you know that Jesus called us His friends? How much did Jesus love us? He loved us so much that He literally laid down His life for us. As a friend, would you lay down your life for your friends? Jesus said not many people would.

We need to remember to be like Jesus. He wants us to be a responsible friend just like He is responsible towards us.

> Parents: Copy the friendship reminder and each day take two of the character traits and talk to your son about how they should be applied towards his life.

TASK: This week talk with dad or mom about the friendship list. What examples can you give of being fair, respecting others, having integrity, being an example, behaving nicely, your duty towards your friends, sharing, having honor, ignoring wrongs, and praising others ?

When you are around your friends this week, remember to put to good use the friendship reminder list.

For who hath known the mind of the Lord, that he may instruct
him? But we have the mind of Christ.
1 Corinthians 2:16

Week Ten

Responsible in Mind

Responsibility & Your Mind

Do you remember the Scripture which told us to love God with ALL our MINDS? What is your mind? It is the spot where you think.

What do you think about?

Ben thinks about many things. He thinks about God, his family, his school and all the things he likes to do.

What does it mean, then, to love God with ALL of our minds?

Just this, God wants to be first in our thoughts. He wants us to remember Him and think about Him daily! He doesn't want to be last on our list, He wants to be the first!

In order to help Ben love God with all of his mind, Ben's dad has been teaching him how to read the book that tells us all about God.

I'm sure that you already know this book. It is called the Bible!

The Bible tells us everything about God. It tells us what God likes, what God loves, and what God does not like. This book is a guide for us. If we read the Bible we can learn to know and love God.

Best of all, the Bible can help our minds be full of God's ways rather than the ways of the world. Many people in the world do not follow God's ways. Their thoughts are different from the way God thinks. This is why God told us to love HIM with all of our minds. He knew that there would be a world who didn't really know Him or love Him, so He gave us the Bible.

To become a responsible man of God, you must start to learn the Bible. That is what this lesson is all about.

Let Your Light Shine!

Parents: Find a child's Bible that is suitable to your child's reading age and get them started in the habit of reading their Bible every day. It is up to you and your discretion on how much they should read, but try to be consistant.

TASK: This week ask dad or mom to start reading your Bible with you. It is very important that you plan with them how much you are to read your Bible each day. Whether it is a verse, a chapter, or a whole book of the Bible, you must make it a part of your life. Plan on reading a portion of it every day that you are alive. The Bible is your spiritual food for your mind. Without it your spirit will starve!

See pages 127-130 for "<u>Read the Bible Through in One Year</u>" Chart.

Lessons in Responsibility

And you who were sometime alienated and enemies in your mind by wicked works, yet now hath he reconciled.
Colossians 1:21

Week Eleven

Responsibility & What You Put in Your Mind

In our last lesson we learned that the most important thing we can put in our mind is the knowledge of God. Where do we find out about God? Right! From the Bible!

We have a responsibility towards God to make sure that we feed ourselves spiritual food, which is God's Word, every day.

We must also be careful to watch what

we allow to come into our minds.

What is an education? Are you being educated?

Yes! Your parents are giving you the education that they believe you need.

Ben's parents are teaching him that the most important thing to learn is the Bible. His parents are teaching him to read the Bible daily.

Ben is also learning to read, write and do arithmetic. Someday Ben will grow up, just like you, and will have a job. He will need this job to take care of a family and a wife of his own. God says that this is very good.

We must be very careful that we have only knowledge that is pleasing to God going into our brains.

The Bible tells us:

"Let no man deceive himself. If any man among you seemeth to be wise in this world, let him become a fool, that he may be wise. For the wisdom of this world is

foolishness with God." 1 Cor. 3:18-19

Can you think of things that go into our minds that might be harmful to them?

1. Unkind thoughts or ideas.

2. Movies that are violent or have unclean content.

3. Sarcastic or nasty jokes.

4. Disobedient thoughts.

5. Music that makes you think bad thoughts or makes you wild and hyper.

6. Coarse or rude comments that may seem funny to other kids, but that you know are not right.

7. You think of three more things...

TASK: This week take a good look around at what you are putting into your mind. At the end of the week, with your parent's help, write down some of the things that you have seen or heard that might not be pleasing to God. Remember the sources so you can be more careful.

Lessons in Responsibility

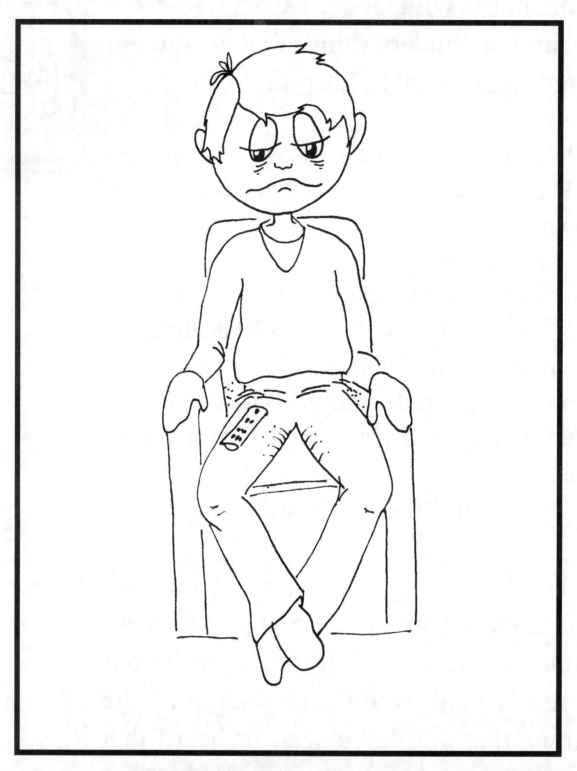

I will set no wicked thing before mine eyes; I hate the work of
them that turn aside; it shall not cleave to me.
Psalms 101:3

Week Twelve

Responsible
in
Mind

Responsibility & The TV

Last week we talked about being careful of what we allow to go into our minds.

Ben has a television in his home. His parents have been very careful regarding what he is allowed to watch.

Do you know the ten commandments that God has given us to live our lives by?

If we know these commandments, we can ask ourselves if anything that we are watching goes against these commands. If

they are, then we know that the show on TV would not be pleasing to God, and therefore we shouldn't be watching it. A responsible person is able to see that something is wrong and decide not to watch that program! They TURN IT OFF!

Here are the Ten Commandments.

1. You shall have no other gods before me.

2.   You shall not make unto thee any graven image, or any likeness of anything that is in heaven above, or that is in the earth beneath, or that is in the water under the earth. You shall not bow down thyself to them, nor serve them; for I the Lord thy God am a jealous God, visiting the sins of the fathers upon the children unto the third and fourth generation of them that hate me; and showing mercy to thousands of them that love me, and keep my commandments.

3. *You shall not take the name of the Lord thy God in vain.*

4. *Remember the sabbath day to keep it holy.*

5. *Honor your father and your mother; that your days may be long upon the land which the Lord your God giveth you.*

6. *Thou shalt not kill.*

7. *You shall not commit adultery.*

8. *You shall not steal.*

9 *You shall not bear false witness against thy neighbor (lying).*

10. *You shall not covet. (Want what others have, envy.) - Exodus 20:3-17*

I will set no wicked thing before my eyes.

Parents, it may be easier to memorize the 2nd commandment by only having them recite, "You shall not make unto thee any graven image."

TASK: Take all this week to memorize the ten commandments. Learning to be responsible means learning to live by God's Word. Knowing God's commandments is a very important part of growing up. If we follow these rules of God, we will be happy and content! God loves us so much that He gave us these commandments to live by!

Lessons in Responsibility

So teach us to number our days, that we may
apply our hearts unto wisdom.
Psalms 90:12

Week Thirteen

Responsible
in
Mind

Responsibility & Video Games

Does your family have video games for you to play with?

Ben's older brothers and sister have had video games since they first started making them. Ben's parents found out that they had to be very careful regarding what they allowed their children to play.

If you are allowed to play video games, you must learn to be very responsible in your choice of games.

First, you must learn how to be disci-

plined regarding how much time you allow yourself to spend on games.

The Bible says, "Teach us to number our days, O, Lord."

What does this mean to you?

Ben has decided that he doesn't want to spend all of his life sitting down in front of the TV playing video games. He has found out that by limiting himself to just one half hour each day, he had enough time to enjoy a short game.

You, too, need to decide how much time you think is *good* for you to be sitting in front of the game cube.

Here are some things to consider as you make your decision:

1. TV and video games steal your life. You are only sitting and not really living when you are involved with them.

2. There are things in many video games which break God's commandments. One of the main

Parents, discuss with your child the importance of making each minute count in their life. Teach them not to waste it on frivolous activities. Instead, encourage them to live a life serving the Lord and others.

rules broken all the time is "You shall not kill."

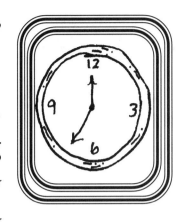

God is really serious about these things. Jesus told us if we even think about doing them in our hearts, then we have already done them. You can say that this is only pretend, but God doesn't look at things this way. This is why you have to be very careful and become responsible towards your Heavenly Father. He sees. He knows. And He wants you to love Him just as He loves you. Jesus said, "If you love me you will obey my commandments."

Parents, it is so important that we teach our children to make their own decisions regarding right and wrong. Some-day mom and dad won't be there to make the rules for them and if we never teach them to have rules for themselves, they won't know how to become responsible.

TASK: Make a decision this week. How much time you are going to allow yourself to watch TV or to play your video games? You may decide not to turn it on at all, or maybe only once a week. Ask dad or mom what they think. You can do this! You are becoming so responsible!

The LOVE of money is the root of **all** evil.
1 Timothy 6:10

Week Fourteen

Responsibility & Money

This is just an introductory lesson on something that you will have to deal with all of your life.

MONEY...

The Bible tells us that the LOVE of money is the root of all evil.

This is a very important warning to us. We are not to love money. This is forbidden. If we obey this teaching, we can learn to make money, handle money and use it as Jesus would want us to use it wisely. We just have to remember, we are not to LOVE it.

How does a young man like you get money? How does your dad get money? How are you going to get money when you are older?

You probably are going to get a job. Then you will earn money for the work that you do.

Ben has some money that he has earned from weeding his parent's garden. He has $2. So, he has a choice. He can either spend that money on something, or he can save that money until the following week when he can earn another $2. How much money will he have altogether if he waits and saves the money? Yes, he would have $4.

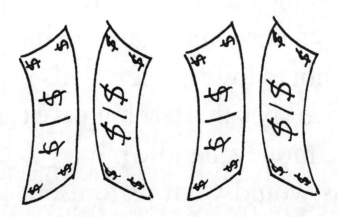

TASK: Here is a little lesson that you and your parents can do together:

1. Ask your parents if you can have a quarter each day this week. You are to put the quarter in your pocket and take it with you wherever you go.

2. You have a choice each day. You can spend your quarter, or you can save it.

3. At the end of the week sit down with your parents and bring out how much money you have left.

4. Did you save any of the money? If you did, did you notice that your money doubles? If you saved all your money, you would have 7 times more than what you started with!

Extra task: Figure this out: You do yard work each day, five times a week. You are paid a $1 each day. How much money will you make in one week? In two weeks? In three weeks? In one month?

He that is faithful in that which is least is faithful also in much;
and he that is unjust in the least is unjust also in much.
Luke 16:10

Week Fifteen

Responsibility & Handling Money

Ben has just gotten to the point where his parents are giving him an allowance. An allowance is an allotment of money given each week. His weekly amount is $1.

Last week we learned how our money doubles, triples and more when we save it. However, Ben wants to spend some of his allowance each week. This is fine, but he needs to learn to save some of it and to place that portion in a long-term piggy

bank.

Ben's parents are encouraging him to give ten (10) cents a week to God as his tithe (we will discuss this in a moment). Another ten (10) cents go into his long-term piggy bank. This means that he has 80 cents left. Ben will put half of this into another short term piggy bank, (40 cents), because he is saving up to buy a new skate board.

TASK: Ask your dad and mom if you may have an allowance. Allowances are a great way to teach good money management. Once your parents give you your money, it is important that you learn right now how to separate it out:

1. TITHE: God told his chosen people to give 10% of their earnings to Him. To give to Him could mean today to give to the poor, to widows, to orphans or missions work. So you must place 10% of

---

your money into a tithe box. If your allowance is a $1, you will give 10 cents of it away to God. This is the most important part of your handling money... the tithe. Remember, God LOVES a cheerful giver, and that you are not to LOVE money! Actually, you have 45 cents in your hand, and after you give 10 cents to the Lord, you will have 35 cents to spend on whatever you would like to!

2. Put 10% of the amount in your long-term piggy bank. (If you get $1 it will be 10 cents.)

3. Take half of the remaining amount and place it in your short term piggy bank.

Lessons in Responsibility

The way of the Lord is strength to the upright.
Proverbs 10:29

Week Sixteen

Responsible
in
Strength

Responsibility & Loving God With ALL Your Strength

You are learning a lot of ways to become responsible! Are you still making your bed every day and keeping on track with your steps? It takes a big, disciplined young man to become responsible.

What does it mean to love God with ALL your strength?

You can have dad or mom read the definition of the word strength in the left margin.

To love God with ALL your strength is to love God with <u>ALL your body</u>.

How will you love God with ALL your body? Do you think it has something to do with what you will *do* with your body? What do you think God want us to do with our bodies?

STRENGTH: That property or quality of a body by which it is enabled to move itself or other bodies. We say, a sick man has not strength to walk, or to raise his head or his arm. We say, a man has strength to life a weight or to draw it. This quality is called also power and force. But force is also used to denote the effect of strength exerted, or the quantity of motion.

The Bible says, "I beseech you therefore, brethren, by the mercies of God, that you present your bodies as a living sacrifice, holy, acceptable unto God, which is your reasonable service." Romans 12:1

What does this mean to you?

Do you know what it means to sacrifice something? It means to willingly give up

something. We are to give our bodies to God and allow God to use us. We are to be His holy people. We are to serve God while we are alive on earth.

The rest of that verse is very important to us too! It says, "And be not conformed to this world; but be you transformed by the renewing of your mind, that you may prove what is that good, and acceptable, and perfect, will of God."

How do you renew your mind so that your body can live for God? By reading the handbook, our guide book, the Bible! If you read the Bible, it will tell you what God wants you to do with your body.

TASK: Sit down with dad or mom and have them read with you Matthew 25:31-46. Discuss with your parents why it is important to Jesus that we DO the Word of God with our bodies, and not just hear about it only.

But I keep under my body, and bring it into subjection; lest that by any means, when I have preached to others, I myself should be a castaway.
1 Corinthians 10:27

Week Seventeen

Responsible in Strength

Responsibility & Your Physical Body

Your physical body is very important to God. Did you know that God calls your body His Temple?

He does: "Know you not that you are the temple of God, that the Spirit of God dwelleth in you? If any man defile the temple of God, him shall God destroy, for the temple of God is holy, which temple you are." 1 Cor. 3:16-17

That's a pretty strong scripture, isn't it? Our bodies belong to the Lord, not to ourselves.

How do you think God wants you to take care of your body, His Temple?____

Ben used to watch way too much TV and played way too many video games. Because he never used his body, it began to get very weak.

Since he has been learning to make good choices for the Lord, and has been learning to do what God wants him to do rather than what HE wants to do, he has gotten much stronger! Since he now limits sedentary activities (like video games) that do not move his body, he is a new person!

It's time to check out your own body. With your parent's help answer these questions:

1. Do you play outside or get some form of activity for more than one hour a day?

2. Do you like to play sports?

3. Do you take breaks and walk around after you have been sitting for a while?

4. Do you choose fruits over sweets?

5. Do you stop eating when you are full?

If you have answered "no" to more than two of these questions, you may need to change the way you have been using and taking care of your body. In the next few lessons, Ben is going to show you better ways to take care of that temple!

TASK: Talk with mom and dad about a plan to improve the way you care for your body. This week, try to stay away from sweets. This means sugary foods. You can do it!

Lessons in Responsibility

What? Know you not that your body is the temple of the Holy
Ghost which is in you, which you have of God and you are not
your own? Therefore glorify God in your body, and in your
spirit, which are God's.
1 Corinthians 6:19-20

Week Eighteen

Responsible
in
Strength

Responsibility & Taking Care of Your Temple

Did you know that you are marvelously made? Your body has over 206 bones, and over 650 muscles in it. Imagine how smart our Heavenly Father is to have put us together so perfectly! It is up to us to take care of our bodies the best way we can.

Ben was sick last year. He had a temperature over 102 and was put to bed for a week as he got better.

The doctor told him that he had caught a flu. This means that he had come into contact with germs, you know those tiny bugs that we can't see? The doctor also said that Ben had not drank enough water. He also didn't eat good food that his mother had cooked for him at meals. This hurt his body and caused it to become weak.

Did you know that the Bible tells us to wash our hands? God knew there were germs and He told his children that they were to wash their hands before they ate and after they touched anything. Do you remember to wash your hands?

This week, we are going to learn some ways that will help us care of our bodies.

1. Remember to always wash your hands before you eat, and after you go to the bathroom. This stops the spread of dirty germs which get us sick.

2. Drink at least eight (8) regular size glasses of water a day. Did you know children need more water than adults? It's true. This is because they are more active.

3. Always brush your teeth and floss after every time you eat. This also helps to keep you healthy. If you don't you can have terrible germs which get trapped in between your teeth on decaying food pieces.

Parents, please help your children to become independently responsible. You may want to gently remind them to do these things this week with a picture of a glass of water, or a WASH HANDS sign placed on the mirror's bathroom. This way they feel they are doing it all by themselves!

TASK: This week try to remember to wash your hands; drink your water; and brush and floss your teeth every day. Make this a new habit! You are taking care of God's Temple and He really likes it when you do this! Add this to your chore list.

"But you, when you fast, anoint thine head, and wash thy face..."
Matthew 6: 17

Week Nineteen

Responsible in Strength

Responsibility & Keeping Your Body Clean

Ben is only seven right now, but he has lived with his older brothers and he will be the first to tell you, that boy, can boys have body odor! Ben has already decided to make sure that he does all that he can so he won't smell.

God made boys to have certain hormones in their bodies that get rid of toxins and poisons in their bodies through

sweat. Actually, it is good that their bodies sweat, as it is showing that their bodies are working.

However, it's a bit hard on others around them, unless you learn how to keep your body clean.

Ben has some new steps that he is going to share with you so that you will always smell pleasant to others:

1. Always take a bath each evening before you go to bed. This washes off all the dirt and grime from the day's work.

2. Use a washcloth and scrub every part of your body with soap. Don't forget to wash behind your ears and under your arms.

3. Wash your hair and make sure to get all the soap out when you rinse.

4. After taking a bath, always wash out the tub and clean up after yourself.

5. Brush your hair and make sure to look nice. Use moisturizing lotion on your body if you have dry skin. Ask dad to show you how.

Turn to page 131 for a Hygiene Chart to follow.

TASK: This week, make it a new habit to take a bath every night and get all the dirt and germs off of your body. Make sure to always pick up after you make a mess. You are learning to be so responsible!

I counsel thee to buy of me gold tried in the fire, that thou
mayest be rich; and white raiment (clothing), that thou may be
clothed,...
Revelation 3:18

Week Twenty

Responsibility & Keeping Your Body Groomed

How do you think Ben looks today? Doesn't he look fine? He dressed all by himself! He picked out his shirt, pants, socks, and shoes, and everything matches just great!

How are you at dressing and taking care of yourself? I bet you do a great job too!

In this lesson we're going to work a little bit on how we prepare to go out into the

world each day.

Have you ever heard the story of King Nebuchadnezzar? He was punished by God, and the Bible tells us that he ate grass like oxen, his hair grew like eagles' feathers, and his nails were like birds' claws.

Daniel 4:28-33

Do you want to look like that? No, of course you don't. Let's learn how to groom ourselves properly.

1. You need to have a hair cut every 4-6 weeks, depending on how fast your hair grows.

2. You should clip your nails every other week. Have dad or mom teach you how to clip them straight across.

3. Wear clean underwear and socks daily, and make sure that the clothes you wear are clean.

4. When choosing your clothing, pick colors that match. Ask mom or dad to help you learn how to match colors.

Your morning ritual after cleaning your room:

1. Pick out your clothes and dress.

2. In the bathroom brush and floss your teeth, wash your face with a washcloth (hanging it up afterward), and comb your hair.

3. If you like some of the deodorant sprays on the market today, use just one squirt. Too much would make everyone around you faint!

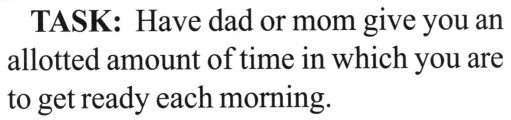

TASK: Have dad or mom give you an allotted amount of time in which you are to get ready each morning.

You might want to use a calendar and write down when you need a hair cut or to clip your nails, as sometimes these things get overlooked.

This week work on your new morning routine or chore chart.

Turn to page 130 for a new helpful Daily Routine Chart.

When thou sittest to eat with a ruler, consider diligently what is
before thee; and put a knife to thy throat, if thou be a man
given to appetite. Be not desirous of his dainties;
for they are deceitful meat.
Proverbs 23:1-3

Week Twenty-One

Responsibility & What You Put into Your Body

Ben has just learned how to slice fruit all by himself. He has started eating fruit and vegetables for snacks rather than sweets, and he loves it!

Ben has learned that God cares what we put into our bodies. Your body is like an engine. It needs fuel. That fuel is the food we eat. If we put bad fuel in our bodies, our bodies will run poorly. If we put good

fuel in our bodies, they will run great! Here are some examples of good food:

· Breads, cereals, rice and pasta
· Vegetables
· Fruits
· Milk, yogurt and cheese
· Meats, poultry, fish, dry beans and peas, eggs, and nuts

These foods cause your body to become stronger and to grow. There are other foods that are not so good for your body. Sugar, white processed foods, boxed foods with preservatives, and fast foods.

Ben has learned how to make a healthy snack, and you can do it too:

APPLES WITH HONEY & CREAM CHEESE

· 1 apple, sliced & cored. Have child use an apple corer/slicer if you have one.
· 1 cup softened cream cheese
· 1/4 cup honey

Place the softened cream cheese and honey in a medium size bowl. Whip together with a fork or whisk.

Serve on a plate with apples & dip in a bowl. It's great!

Parents, our Home Economics Level 1 teaches how to cook & clean in a more in-depth study if you are interested in more healthy ideas.

TASK: This week plan on making healthy choices to snack on for you and your family. Some ideas are popcorn, celery with cream cheese spread, tortilla chips & dip, crackers with peanut butter, peeled carrots, or orange slices. Make at least five snacks this week, all by yourself. You choose.

Lessons in Responsibility

The slothful man saith, There is a lion in the way; a lion is in the streets. As the door turneth upon his hinges, so doth the slothful upon his bed. The slothful hideth his hand in his bosom; it grieveth him to bring it again to his mouth.
Proverbs 26:13-15

Week Twenty-Two

Responsible in Strength

Responsibility & Exercising God's Temple

Ben loves to jump rope! Have you ever jumped rope before? It is so much fun, and it's even more fun when he has others to jump rope with him.

What do you like to do? Run, skateboard, hike, swim, walk, stretch, ski, shoot baskets, sled, surf, boogie board?

There are so many things that we can do to keep our temple in good shape.

You know that God wants you to take good care of your body. After all, it *is* His temple!

It is very important that you stretch your body and exercise it each and every day.

Ben has learned some following stretches:

1. This stretch is great for your legs & back:

Twist & Stretch

2. Here's a stretch for your sides and arms.

stretch one side then the other

3. This one is for your torso & back.

Touch your toes!

Stretching is great to do before you exercise. This week, why don't you pick your favorite activity and plan on exercising daily.

Choose from the following & do daily:

Parents, there is no better age than 6-7 to get children in the habit of being active. This will stay with them all of their lives and save them from ailments that non-athletes suffer from..

Running   Skateboarding

Biking   Basketball

Lessons in Responsibility

Put on therefore, as the elect of God, holy and beloved, bowels of mercies, kindness, humbleness of mind, meekness, longsuffering; and above all these things, put on charity, which is the bond of perfectness.
Colossians 3:12, 14

Week Twenty-Three

Responsible in Strength

Responsibility & Helping Others with Your Strength

We have learned that our bodies are to be used for God's glory. We are to live for Him daily. We do this by helping others here on earth. The Bible says that when we help others, we are really helping Jesus!

Remember the Scripture we read about the sheep and the goats? We are going to be sheep & serve our Jesus!

Lessons in Responsibility

A Helping Hand

There are many people who need help all around us.

Ben has a neighbor who lives all alone. He started talking to him and now they visit regularly. He helps him any way he can.

What can you do to help others? Here are some ideas:

Parents, the only way our children learn to be kind, loving and considerate of others is if we teach them to do so. Help them to volunteer while they are little and it will become second nature to them when they are older.

· Visit your elderly neighbors & see if they need any help.

· Visit your local nursing home and ask if there is anyone who would like to play a game or just talk.

· Record a children's book and give it to the children's ward at your local hospital.

· Pick up litter that others leave.

· Grow a garden and give your produce to your neighbors or elderly that you know.

TASK: Can you think of something that you know you can do to help someone else? This week, work on trying to do just one thing for someone who is in need. It can even be to walk someone's dog! You decide. I bet you can come up with something all on your own!

Lessons in Responsibility

That you might walk worthy of the Lord unto all pleasing,
being fruitful in every good work,
and increasing in the knowledge of God.
Colossians 1:10

Week Twenty-four

Responsibility & Your Chores

Did you know one of the ways you can become a responsible person is to do chores? Yes! Chores are one of the best things possible for you. Chores help you to become considerate towards others by teaching you doing your share. They teach you to be thoughtful of others. They also teach you to become grown up and independent! If you don't have chores, you may become lazy and irresponsible. God wants you to grow up happy and healthy by obeying His ways.

Ben has a few daily chores that he does. He likes helping around the house. God loves it when we do good towards others. We are helping our family by making a clean and better place to live.

Besides his morning routine, he is responsible for the following chores. Maybe you might want to take on these chores at your house!

1. Unloading the silverware in the dishwasher.

2. Folding his own clothes, towels and washcloths.

3. Watering certain plants.

4. Dusting his room and the family room.

Parents, being consistent with a chore list is so important. Make a list where they can see it and designate chores for certain days. Help them to follow through and it will soon become a habit for them.

TASK: There are many things that you can do to help around the house. Ask dad or mom what they want your chores to be. Maybe you might want to review and add to the chores you already have. Here are some more ideas to help: Set the table; vacuum; make a cereal breakfast; make a sandwich lunch; take out the garbage; feed your pet; clean the tub & sink; take the groceries in; sweep the kitchen floor; sweep your porches; shovel snow...

For even when we were with you, this we commanded you,
that if any would not work, neither should he eat.
2 Thessalonians 3:10

Week Twenty-Five

Responsible
in
Strength

Responsibility & Home Maintenance

Ben helps his dad take care of his home. He's learning so much and someday he will be able to take care of his own home, too!

There is an awful lot to learn. He and his dad have been working outside in the yard and fixing the fences. They are keeping the house in good repair by painting it, fixing the calking around tubs and sinks, and much more! There's a lot for a boy

to do to take care of a house!

What do you do to help your dad around the house? Can you name a few things right now?

How about fixing things? Are you good at that?

One major thing that usually needs to be checked around the home, is that all the screws are tightened once a year.

Do you know what a screwdriver is? How about a hammer? They are a man's best friend. Here are the basic tools you need:

1. A FLAT screwdriver. This means the head is flat.

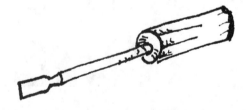

2. A regular screwdriver. This means it has a star shaped head.

3. A hammer. You use this to hammer nails.

TASK: With your dad's (mom's) supervision, this week complete some of the following tasks:

1. If you have a fence around your house, hammer in any loose boards.

2. Check to see if any screws are loose around your doors and screw them in tightly.

3. With dad watching, check to see if the light switch panels are screwed on tightly.

4. If you have a skateboard or a snowboard, check to see if the screws are in tight.

5. Ask dad if he has some things that he needs you to fix that aren't on the list.

Lessons in Responsibility

And when you liest down, you shall not be afraid; yes, you
shall lie down,
and your sleep shall be sweet.
Proverbs 3:24

Week Twenty-Six

Responsible in Strength

Responsibility & Getting Enough Rest

Here's a picture of Ben settling down in his comfy bed. He does it all on his own. But I have to tell you, he didn't always do this. He used to fuss, cry, make excuses, or want something to eat! He'd do anything to delay going to bed.

All that changed when he found out how important it was for him to get rest and

what rest does for you.

Did you know that God made your body to sleep? Your body needs 10 hours of sleep each night if you are six or seven years old. If you don't get the amount of sleep you need, you can wear your body down and get sick easily, not to mention becoming a grump!

Ben is now on a bedtime schedule and feels much better! Why don't you try it too?

1. After bath, Ben picks out his PJ's that he likes to wear. (Sometimes he likes the soft flannel ones that are really snugly.)

2. Next, he turns on soft music, or his Bible tapes, and lies down in his bed.

3. After listening for 15 minutes or so, he turns off his tape player and light and goes back to bed.

4. Dad or mom comes into the room and says his prayers with him. Soon he is fast asleep, dreaming good dreams.

TASK: This week, try this bedtime routine every night. At first, you might have trouble falling asleep right away, but the more you do it, the easier it will become. Make sure that you go to bed early enough so you get your 10 hours of sleep!

He that keeps the commandments keepeth his own soul;
but he that despises His ways shall die.
Proverbs 19:16

Week Twenty-Seven

Responsible in Soul

Responsibility & Loving God with ALL our Soul

What is a soul? The dictionary tells us that our soul is the spiritual, rational and immortal substance in man. In simple terms, our soul is our spirit. Our spirit is eternal. When you love Jesus, your physical body may give out, or die, but the inside *you*, your spirit, will live forever.

God wants you to love him with ALL your spirit or soul. Every bit of it.

Did you know that you were created to be with God? In the beginning, God created Adam and Eve, and God walked with them in the Garden of Eden. Genesis 3:8

It was when sin entered the world, through disobedience, that we became separated from God and were kicked out of the garden. Genesis 3:22-24

Jesus made a way for us to be able to have fellowship with God again when he died for us. 2 Corinthians 5:18-19

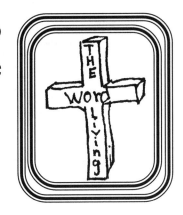

Then a miracle happened! God made Jesus alive again after he had died for us! Now, if you love Jesus and believe that he died and rose again, all the bad stuff that you do, your sins, are forgiven. Now you can talk to God! No more are you separated from Him. All through our wonderful Jesus! Ephesians 1:3-23

TASK: Read about the Good News, sometimes called The Gospel. It is the Good News of how we are no longer separated from God! Hebrews 9:8-15 Talk with your parents about John 3:16.

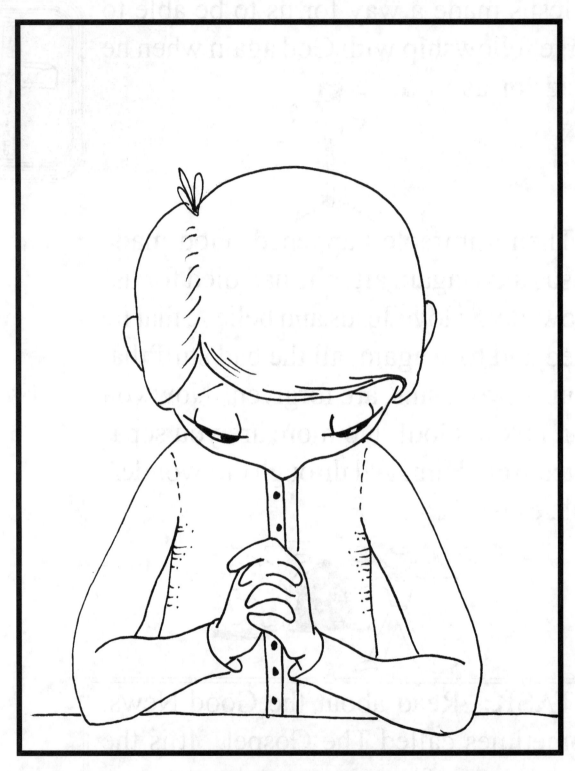

Pray without ceasing.
1 Thessalonians 5:17

Week Twenty-Eight

Responsibility & Your Relationship With God

What is talking to God called? It is called prayer.

Ben loves to talk to God. He gets up in the morning, smiles and says, "Good morning, Heavenly Father!" When he walks throughout the day he talks to his Heavenly Father in his spirit and thanks him for the things he has. You can talk to God

any time.

Do you like to talk to God? Talking to our Heavenly Father is like talking to the one who loves you more than anyone else in creation. He wants you to talk with Him. He'll talk to you, too. Some people call His voice the "still, quiet voice". Other people call it your "conscience".

You will get to recognize His voice. Jesus said, "And when he putteth forth his own sheep, he goes before them, and the sheep follow him; for they know his voice." John 10:4

God wants a relationship with you. He wants you to love Him with ALL your soul. When you love someone you will

want to spend time with them. This is what you do when you pray.

TASK: How do you get started talking to God? Here's some easy suggestions:

1. First thing in the morning, smile and tell your Heavenly Father, "Good morning", and tell Him thank you for the day.

2. Throughout your day, think of God and just talk to Him like you would anyone else. Tell Him about your struggles or the things that you are really happy about.

3. At nighttime, when you are laying in your bed trying to go to sleep, talk to God during this time and tell Him thank you for everything that He has done for you, and to ask for guidance.

4. God wants you to ask Him for all that you need. The Bible tells us to "knock" and the door will be opened to you. If you ask God to speak to you, He will. He promises! Don't stop praying.

Enter into His gates with thanksgiving, and into His courts with praise. Be thankful unto Him and bless His name!
Psalms 100:4

Week Twenty-Nine

Responsible in Soul

Responsibility & Having a Thankful Spirit

What are you thankful for? Do you have parents who love you? A home? A cozy bed? Running water? Food to eat? Friends to play with?

Where do all these blessings come from?

Yes, God. He is the one from whom all blessings flow.

Did you know that God wants you to live your life being thankful? The Bible tells us that there are people who know

God, but they do not glorify Him as God and they are not thankful. Because of this they become vain in their imaginations and their foolish hearts are darkened. <small>Romans 1:21</small>

Ben decided that he was never going to be unthankful. He wants to live his life always thanking God for everything!

What happens when you are thankful for everything that comes your way? You are happy and joyful. You are content with what you have. You won't be greedy, or selfish, or discontent!

This lesson is a very important lesson. One of the biggest responsibilities you have is to thank your Heavenly Father for everything He has given you.

The Bible tells us to give thanks *always* for *all* things to God and the Father in the name of our Lord Jesus Christ. <small>Ephesians 5:20</small>

TASK: How do you show God and people around you that you are thankful? Remember last week's lesson? You need to talk to our Heavenly Father and thank Him. Here's some helpful tips:

1. Thank God when bad or sad things happen because He can turn them to good.

2. Thank God when your parents punish you because this means they love you.

3. Thank God when you have good things happen to you, it's all from Him.

4. Thank God when you think something is a coincidence, as there is no such thing as a coincidence or accident. God is in control of everything.

5. Thank God for every minute you spend with loved ones and family. You need to appreciate them while you have them here with you.

6. Thank God for good memories, for even our loved ones who have died live forever in our memory.

7. Thank God for being God. Tell Him how wonderful He is and how thankful you are for Him. Always be thankful!

Parents, Psalms 100 & Psalms 103 are so encouraging. Please take time this week to read these passages with your son.

Continue in prayer, and watch in the same with thanksgiving.
Colossians 4:2

Week Thirty

Responsible in Soul

Review of the Responsibilities that You have Learned

Well, you have done it! You have finished this whole book and have learned so many different things. You and Ben are going to be such responsible young men!

Did you know that when you are responsible, people trust you? When people trust you, you usually are given more privileges. I bet your parents are going to allow you to do many more things now, all by yourself!

Just for review, let's go over some of the topics that you have studied.

QUESTIONS:

~What are the four things you are to love God with?

~What are your household rules?

~Is your room still organized?

~How often do you change your sheets and make your bed?

~What is your morning routine?

~What are your responsibilities towards your sister/s?

~Why is it important to obey your parents?

~Do you remember what FRIENDSHIP stands for? (Pg. 38)

~Why is it important to read the Bible?

~Explain why you need to be careful of what you allow into your mind?

~Can you recite the ten (10) commandments?

~How much time do you allow yourself to

watch TV or play video games? (You may choose not to participate at all!)

~Is money evil?

~What does God call your body? (Temple)

~What are your steps that you do when taking your bath? (Pg. 78)

~How often should you cut your hair?

~How often should you clip your nails?

~What are some examples of good food you should eat?

~What is your favorite choice of exercise?

~Are there some things that you have done to help others? What are they?

~What are your daily chores?

~What's the difference between a flat & regular screw driver?

~What time do you go to bed?

Wow! You sure have learned to be responsible.

Ben thanks you for learning along with him, and wants you to remember to keep up with all that you have learned.

Congratulations on a job well done!

Lessons in Responsibility

Daily Routine

	Monday	Tuesday	Wednesday	Thursday	Friday
Make Bed					
Put Clothes Up					
Clean Room					
Wash Face					
Brush Teeth					
Comb Hair					
Clean Bathroom					

☙ Level One ❧

Read the Bible Through in One Year

Month 1	Month 2	Month 3	Month 4
1= Genesis 1-3	1 = Leviticus 1-4	1 = Deuteronomy 5-7	1 = 1 Samuel 11-13
2 = Genesis 4-7	2 = Leviticus 5-7	2 = Deuteronomy 8-10	2 = 1 Samuel 14, 15
3 = Genesis 8-11	3 = Leviticus 8, 9	3 = Deuteronomy 11-13	3 = 1 Samuel 16, 17
4 = Genesis 12-15	4 = Leviticus 10-12	4 = Deuteronomy 14-17	4 = 1 Samuel 18-20
5 = Genesis 16-18	5 = Leviticus 13	5 = Deuteronomy 18-20	5 = 1 Samuel 21-24
6 = Genesis 19-20	6 = Leviticus 14, 15	6 = Deuteronomy 21-23	6 = 1 Samuel 25-27
7 = Genesis 21-23	7 = Leviticus 16-18	7 = Deuteronomy 24-26	7 = 1 Samuel 28-31
8 = Genesis 24, 25	8 = Leviticus 19-21	8 = Deuteronomy 27, 28	8 = 2 Samuel 1-3
9 = Genesis 26-28	9 = Leviticus 22, 23	9 = Deuteronomy 29-31	9 = 2 Samuel 4-7
10 = Genesis 29, 30	10 = Leviticus 24, 25	10 = Deuteronomy 32-34	10 = 2 Samuel 8-11
11 = Genesis 31, 32	11 = Leviticus 26, 27	11 = Joshua 1-4	11 = 2 Samuel 12, 13
12 = Genesis 33-35	12 = Numbers 1-2	12 = Joshua 5-7	12 = 2 Samuel 14, 15
13 = Genesis 36-38	13 = Numbers 3, 4	13 = Joshua 8, 9	13 = 2 Samuel 16, 17
14 = Genesis 39-41	14 = Numbers 5, 6	14 = Joshua 10, 11	14 = 2 Samuel 18, 19
15 = Genesis 42-44	15 = Numbers 7	15 = Joshua 12-14	15 = 2 Samuel 20-22
16 = Genesis 45-47	16 = Numbers 8-10	16 = Joshua 15-17	16 = 2 Samuel 23, 24
17 = Genesis 48-50	17 = Numbers 11-13	17 = Joshua 18-20	17 = 1 Kings 1
18 = Exodus 1-3	18 = Numbers 14, 15	18 = Joshua 21, 22	18 = 1 Kings 2, 3
19 = Exodus 4-6	19 = Numbers 16-18	19 = Joshua 23, 24	19 = 1 Kings 4-6
20 = Exodus 7-9	20 = Numbers 19-21	20 = Judges 1-3	20 = 1 Kings 7
21 = Exodus 10-12	21 = Numbers 22-24	21 = Judges 4-6	21 = 1 Kings 8
22 = Exodus 13-15	22 = Numbers 25, 26	22 = Judges 7, 8	22 = 1 Kings 9, 10
23 = Exodus 16-18	23 = Numbers 27-29	23 = Judges 9, 10	23 = 1 Kings 11, 12
24 = Exodus 19-21	24 = Numbers 30, 31	24 = Judges 11-13	24 = 1 Kings 13, 14
25 = Exodus 22-24	25 = Numbers 32, 33	25 = Judges 14-16	25 = 1 Kings 15-17
26 = Exodus 25-27	26 = Numbers 34-36	26 = Judges 17-19	26 = 1 Kings 18, 19
25 = Exodus 28, 29	27 = Deuteronomy 1, 2	27 = Judges 20, 21	27 = 1 Kings 20, 21
28 = Exodus 30-32	28 = Deuteronomy 3, 4	28 = Ruth 1-4	28 = 1 Kings 22, 2 Ki. 1
29 = Exodus 33-35	. . .	29 = 1 Samuel 1-3	29 = 2 Kings 2-4
30 = Exodus 36-38	. . .	30 = 1 Samuel 4-7	30 = 2 Kings 5-7
31 = Exodus 39, 40	. . .	31 = 1 Samuel 8-10	. . .

Lessons in Responsibility

Month 5	Month 6	Month 7	Month 8
1 = 2 Kings 8, 9	**1** = Ezra 9, 10	**1** = Psalms 90-97	**1** = Isaiah 43-47
2 = 2 Kings 10-12	**2** = Nehemiah 1-3	**2** = Psalm 98-104	**2** = Isaiah 48-51
3 = 2 Kings 13, 14	**3** = Nehemiah 4-6	**3** = Psalms 105-107	**3** = Isaiah 52-56
4 = 2 Kings 15, 16	**4** = Nehemiah 7, 8	**4** = Psalms 108-116	**4** = Isaiah 57-59
5 = 2 Kings 17, 18	**5** = Nehemiah 9,10	**5** = Psalms 117-119:72	**5** = Isaiah 60-63
6 = 2 Kings 19, 21	**6** = Nehemiah 11-13	**6** = Psalms 119:73-176	**6** = Isaiah 64-66
7 = 2 Kings 22-25	**7** = Esther 1-3	**7** = Psalms 120-135	**7** = Jeremiah 1-3
8 = 1 Chronicles 1	**8** = Esther 4-7	**8** = Psalms 136-142	**8** = Jeremiah 4-6
9 = 1 Chronicles 2-4	**9** = Esther 8-10	**9** = Psalms 143-150	**9** = Jeremiah 7-9
10 = 1 Chronicles 5, 6	**10** = Job 1-5	**10** = Proverbs 1-4	**10** = Jeremiah 10-12
11 = 1 Chronicles 7-9	**11** = Job 6-10	**11** = Proverbs 5-8	**11** = Jeremiah 13-15
12 = 1 Chronicles 10-12	**12** = Job 11-15	**12** = Proverbs 9-13	**12** = Jeremiah 16-18
13 = 1 Chronicles 13-16	**13** = Job 16-21	**13** = Proverbs 14-17	**13** = Jeremiah 19-22
14 = 1 Chronicles 17-19	**14** = Job 22-28	**14** = Proverbs 18-21	**14** = Jeremiah 23-25:16
15 = 1 Chronicles 20-23	**15** = Job 29-33	**15** = Proverbs 22-24	**15** = Jeremiah 25:17-27
16 = 1 Chronicles 24-26	**16** = Job 34-37	**16** = Proverbs 25-28	**16** = Jeremiah 28-30
17 = 1 Chronicles 27-29	**17** = Job 38-42	**17** = Proverbs 29-31	**17** = Jeremiah 31, 32
18 = 2 Chronicles 1-4	**18** = Psalms 1-9	**18** = Ecclesiastes 1-6	**18** = Jeremiah 33-35
19 = 2 Chronicles 5-7	**19** = Psalms 10-17	**19** = Ecclesiastes 7-12	**19** = Jeremiah 36-38
20 = 2 Chronicles 8-10	**20** = Psalms 18-22	**20** = Song / Solomon 1-8	**20** = Jeremiah 39-41
21 = 2 Chronicles 11-14	**21** = Psalms 23-31	**21** = Isaiah 1-4	**21** = Jeremiah 42-44
22 = 2 Chronicles 15-18	**22** = Psalms 32-37	**22** = Isaiah 5-8	**22** = Jeremiah 45-48
23 = 2 Chronicles 19-22	**23** = Psalms 38-44	**23** = Isaiah 9-12	**23** = Jeremiah 49, 50
24 = 2 Chronicles 23-25	**24** = Psalms 45-51	**24** = Isaiah 13-16	**24** = Jeremiah 51, 52
25 = 2 Chronicles 26-28	**25** = Psalms 52-59	**25** = Isaiah 17-21	**25** = Lamentations 1, 2
26 = 2 Chronicles 29, 30	**26** = Psalms 60-67	**26** = Isaiah 22-25	**26** = Lamentations 3-5
27 = 2 Chronicles 31-33	**27** = Psalms 68-71	**27** = Isaiah 26-28	**27** = Ezekiel 1-4
28 = 2 Chronicles 34, 35	**28** = Psalms 72-77	**28** = Isaiah 29-31	**28** = Ezekiel 5-8
29 = 2 Chron. 36, Ezra 1, 2	**29** = Psalms 78-81	**29** = Isaiah 32-35	**29** = Ezekiel 9-12
30 = Ezra 3-5	**30** = Psalms 82-89	**30** = Isaiah 36-38	**30** = Ezekiel 13-15
31 = Ezra 6-8	. . .	**31** = Isaiah 39-42	**31** = Ezekiel 16

☺ Level One ☺

Month 9	Month 10	Month 11	Month 12
1 = Ezekiel 17-19	**1** = Zechariah 11-14	**1** = Luke 21, 22	**1** = 1 Corinthians 12-14
2 = Ezekiel 20, 21	**2** = Malachi 1-4	**2** = Luke 23, 24	**2** = 1 Corinthians 15, 16
3 = Ezekiel 22, 23	**3** = Matthew 1-4	**3** = John 1-3	**3** = 2 Corinthians 1-4
4 = Ezekiel 24-26	**4** = Matthew 5, 6	**4** = John 4, 5	**4** = 2 Corinthians 5-8
5 = Ezekiel 27, 28	**5** = Matthew 7-9	**5** = John 6, 7	**5** = 2 Corinthians 9-13
6 = Ezekiel 29-31	**6** = Matthew 10-12	**6** = John 8, 9	**6** = Galatians 1-4
7 = Ezekiel 32, 33	**7** = Matthew 13, 14	**7** = John 10, 11	**7** = Gal.5, 6; Eph. 1, 2
8 = Ezekiel 34-36	**8** = Matthew 15-17	**8** = John 12, 13	**8** = Ephesians 3-6
9 = Ezekiel 37, 38	**9** = Matthew 18-20	**9** = John 14-16	**9** = Philippians 1-4
10 = Ezekiel 39, 40	**10** = Matthew 21, 22	**10** = John 17, 18	**10** = Colossians 1-4
11 = Ezekiel 41-43	**11** = Matthew 23, 24	**11** = John 19-21	**11** = 1 Thessalonians 1-4
12 = Ezekiel 44, 45	**12** = Matthew 25, 26	**12** = Acts 1-3	**12** = 1 Thes. 5, 2 Thes. 1-3
13 = Ezekiel 46-48	**13** = Matthew 27, 28	**13** = Acts 4-6	**13** = 1 Timothy 1-4
14 = Daniel 1, 2	**14** = Mark 1-3	**14** = Acts 7, 8	**14** = 1 Timothy 5, 6
15 = Daniel 3, 4	**15** = Mark 4, 5	**15** = Acts 9, 10	**15** = 2 Timothy 1-4
16 = Daniel 5, 6	**16** = Mark 6, 7	**16** = Acts 11-13	**16** = Titus 1-3; Philemon
17 = Daniel 7, 8	**17** = Mark 8, 9	**17** = Acts 14-16	**17** = Hebrews 1-5
18 = Daniel 9, 10	**18** = Mark 10, 11	**18** = Acts 17, 18	**18** = Hebrews 6-9
19 = Daniel 11, 12	**19** = Mark 12, 13	**19** = Acts 19, 20	**19** = Hebrews 10, 11
20 = Hosea 1-6	**20** = Mark 14-16	**20** = Acts 21, 22	**20** = Hebrews 12, 13
21 = Hosea 7-12	**21** = Luke 1	**21** = Acts 23-25	**21** = James 1-5
22 = Hos. 13, 14; Joel 1-3	**22** = Luke 2, 3	**22** = Acts 26-28	**22** = 1 Peter 1-4
23 = Amos 1-5	**23** = Luke 4, 5	**23** = Romans 1-3	**23** = 1 Peter 5; 2 Peter 1-3
24 = Amos 6-9; Obadiah	**24** = Luke 6, 7	**24** = Romans 4-7	**24** = 1 John 1-5
25 = Jonah 1-4, Mic. 1, 2	**25** = Luke 8	**25** = Romans 8-10	**25** = 2 John; 3 John; Jude
26 = Micah 3-7	**26** = Luke 9	**26** = Romans 11-14	**26** = Revelation 1-3
27 = Nahum, Habakkuk	**27** = Luke 10, 11	**27** = Romans 15, 16	**27** = Revelation 4-8
28 = Zephaniah, Haggai	**28** = Luke 12, 13	**28** = 1 Corinthians 1-4	**28** = Revelation 9-12
29 = Zechariah 1-6	**29** = Luke 14-16	**29** = 1 Corinthians 5-8	**29** = Revelation 13-16
30 = Zechariah 7-10	**30** = Luke 17, 18	**30** = 1 Corinthians 9-10	**30** = Revelation 17-19
. . .	**31** = Luke 19, 20	. . .	**31** = Revelation 20-22

Daily Routine 2

	Monday	Tuesday	Wednesday	Thursday	Friday
Make bed					
Put Clothes Up					
Clean Room					
Wash Face					
Brush Teeth					
Floss Teeth					
Comb Hair					
Clean Bathrm					
Deodorant					
Hair Cut					
Nails Clipped					
Clothes Match					

Bath List

	Monday	Tuesday	Wednesday	Thursday	Friday
Bath					
Scrub with Soap					
Wash Face					
Wash Hair					
Dry & Lotion					
Wash Tub					
Clean Bathroom					

ORDER FORM

___Narrow Way Character Curriculum $32.95
(Includes 8 Pearable Kingdom Stories-Are not repeated in Volumes Below)

Pearables Kingdom Stories:
___ Volume 1 $17.50
___ Volume 2 $17.50
___ Volume 3 $17.50

___Narrow Way Character Curriculum & Pearables 1,2, & 3 Volumes SET (listed above) $72.00

___ Personal Help for Boys Text & Workbook $28

___Personal Help for Boys Text Only $22.50
___Personal Help for Boys Workbook Only $11.95 each

Our Hope Chest Series:

___ Volume 1 - Personal Help for Girls $22.50

___ Volume 2 - Preparing Your Hope Chest $22.50

What the Bible Says About...
___ Being a Girl $3.95
___ Being a Boy $3.95

The Quiet Arts Series, <u>Home Economics for Home Schoolers:</u>

___ Level 1 (Ages 6 and up) $18.95
___ Level 2 (Ages 8 and up) $18.95
___ Level 3 (Ages 10 and up) $18.95

___ALL three Levels of Home Economics $48

The Gentleman's Series, <u>Lessons in Responsibility</u>

___ Level 1 (Ages 6 and up) $18.95
___ Level 2 (Ages 8 and up) $18.95

___Subtotal
___ Shipping (Please add $3 for orders under $30. $30 & over please add 10%. Out of U.S. please add 25% of total.)

Name_____

Address_____

City/St/Zip_____

Please mail your purchase order to:

PEARABLES
P.O. Box 272000
Fort Collins, CO 80527

Visit **www.pearables.com** for samples.

Lessons in Responsibility

☻ Level One ☻

☻ Level One ☻

Lessons in Responsibility

☻ Level One ☻

Lessons in Responsibility

🚌 Level One 🚌

🚌

Lessons in Responsibility

☻ Level One ☻

Lessons in Responsibility

Lessons in Responsibility

144